Original title:
Frosty the Drama Queen

Copyright © 2024 Creative Arts Management OÜ
All rights reserved.

Author: Gideon Shaw
ISBN HARDBACK: 978-9916-94-312-0
ISBN PAPERBACK: 978-9916-94-313-7

Winter's Whimsical Diva

In a coat of white so bright,
She prances with delight.
Every gust becomes a show,
Snowy sparkles steal the glow.

With a twirl and a flair,
She dances through the air.
Chilly winds whisper a tease,
While snowflakes drop like confetti with ease.

The Glimmering Snowflake's Serenade

A snowflake lands with grace,
On the nose of a surprised face.
She giggles and gives a wink,
Then twirls, making all think.

Her sparkly gown, a sight to see,
Reflects the light so brilliantly.
With every flurry, she holds the stage,
A diva at every age!

Frostbite's Grand Performance

With icy breath and a cheeky grin,
She struts around, let the fun begin!
Snowflakes join in her parade,
Creating chaos, a perfect charade.

Laughing with glee, she takes a bow,
While snowmen stand in awe somehow.
On this chilly stage of white,
Her frosty antics steal the night.

Melodrama in the Snow

Oh, what a scene, a dramatic play,
As snowflakes fight to steal the display.
With every flurry and every slide,
She laughs and shrieks, full of pride.

Whirling and twirling, a frosty queen,
With props of pine, she's dressed so keen.
The winter's chill, a comedic twist,
In her snowy world, who could resist?

The Glittering Drama

In a world of snowflakes bold,
A character with flair, behold!
With laughter echoing through the air,
She twirls and spins, without a care.

With crystals sparkling in the night,
Her antics bring such pure delight.
She wears a crown of icy grace,
In this grand ice and snow-filled space.

When Snowflakes Weep

The storm clouds gather, what a scene!
As she prepares for her routine.
With a wink and a theatrical sigh,
She makes the snowflakes laugh and cry.

"Oh, how the winter treats me so!"
She wails, with a dramatic flow.
The flurries dance, they swirl and spin,
In her snowy tales, where laughs begin.

The Frosted Curtain Call

As the chandelier of icicles gleams,
She takes her bow, fulfilling dreams.
With a flick of her scarf made of frost,
She acts like a star, never lost.

The audience of squirrels stand in awe,
Each little performance, a great draw.
With each chilly act, she stole the show,
In the frost and the snow, she steals the glow.

Shards of Winter Heartbreak

With melodrama wrapped in white,
She pouts at the stars in the night.
"Oh, icy winds, my heart's a mess!"
Yet giggles follow her bold excess.

But watch out for her tears of snow,
For even her frowns come with a glow.
In the chill, she loves to play,
Making winter brighter every day.

Emotional Icicles

In the cold town square, she makes a scene,
With her twirls and her curls, she's really quite keen.
Snowflakes applaud as they dance to the beat,
While the chill in the air can't compete with her heat.

A spectacle here, an uproarious sight,
She's melting hearts, and it feels just right.
With each icy tear, she crafts a new spark,
Chasing sunshine dreams in the frigid park.

The Tundra Tragedy

In a frosty ballet, she sweeps and she sways,
But her scarf's all knotted in comical ways.
With a flip of her wrist, she reels in the crowd,
Dramatic as ever, bold and quite loud.

A tumble, a slip, and the snowflakes all cheer,
"Oh, what a performance! Let's guffaw here!"
But she'll rise with aplomb, never one to reset,
Endearing the crowd with her chilly vignette.

Artistry in Winter Whispers

With a wink and a grin, she steals every gaze,
Her antics entwined in a wintery haze.
The snowflakes join in, a friend in her jest,
Spinning tales in the frost, she's truly the best.

A cape made of ice and a crown formed of frost,
Though sometimes her lines leave her a bit lost.
Yet laughter erupts like the crack of a freeze,
As she charms all the critters and dashes with ease.

The Pearls Beneath the Snow

Amidst sparkling mounds, she prances with flair,
Each snowball a prop, and she's unaware.
With an eloquent pose, she takes in the crowd,
Her frosty performance, delightfully loud.

"Oh, look at me shine!" she declares with a laugh,
As icicles dangle, a humorous gaffe.
But beneath all the chuckles, the giggles and glee,
Lies a heart made of warmth 'neath the cold, can't you see?

A Shatter of Silver Tears

In a world of icy sparkles bright,
A figure prances, a comical sight.
With flair and a twist, a swooping pose,
Silver tears rolling, but nobody knows.

She storms the stage, a tempest in white,
With scarves a-twirl, oh what a delight!
Her antics cause giggles, laughter and cheer,
As snowflakes dance down, drawing us near.

Pantomime in Crystal

A theater of frost, where shadows play,
With a twinkle of frost, she steals the day.
In dramatic fashion, she slips and she slides,
Winking and giggling, as humor abides.

Her crown made of snow, her gown frozen lace,
She strikes a grand pose, as if running a race.
With each funny fall, the audience roars,
In her crystal cabaret, laughter soars.

Winter's Wallflower Ball

Beneath frosty lights, she takes to the floor,
Chiding the crowd to come join her encore.
With a shimmy and shake, she melts hearts away,
At the winter ball, where the shy come to play.

The snowflakes twirl wildly, she leads them with glee,
A wallflower no more, she's as bold as can be.
A slip here, a fall there, it's part of the fun,
In this frosty affair, where laughter's the run.

Chills and Thrills on Ice

With a dash and a splash, she glides on the freeze,
Performing wild stunts, bringing everyone to knees.
She leaps and she twirls, a mesmerizing spree,
Making even the ice feel a touch of glee.

But oh, what a fumble! She tumbles with flair,
Like a snowball in motion, she lands with a care.
Yet up she springs, laughing, spreading the fun,
A frosty performer, shining like the sun.

The Cold Hearted Diva

In her icy gown, she struts, oh so bold,
With a sparkle that leaves the bravest cold.
Her breath like a blizzard, she steals the show,
While the audience shivers at her frosty glow.

With a flick of her wrist, she commands the scene,
Making critics question what she really means.
Her pouts and her poses, a dramatic tease,
All while the stage crew aim at freezing breeze.

Tinsel Tension

Glistening garlands adorned with flair,
She throws a tantrum, but no one cares.
Wrapped in sparkles, she flails and shines,
Yet backstage whispers bring laughter in lines.

Her strut down the hall is a hilarious sight,
Steam from her breath, a comical fright.
While tinsel falls tangled in her long hair,
She trips and she tumbles, but she's unaware.

Shivering Showstoppers

The curtain will rise, and the cold winds blow,
A troupe of ice dancers ready to go.
With shivers and giggles, they chaotically twirl,
Each pirouette almost sends them to whirl.

They glide and they slip, a clumsy ballet,
In jackets and scarves, they dance in a fray.
With laughter erupting from front to the back,
These frosty performers keep losing their track.

Frigid Confessions

She shivers and shakes, mid-sentence she stutters,
Accusations of frostbite, her drama just sputters.
With fans that are fickle, they laugh and they cheer,
While she claims her heart's cold, we still want her here.

In the spotlight bright, with a glimmering tear,
She flaunts all her woes, but we can't help but sneer.
Her tales are embellished, wrapped up in white,
Yet the humor remains in her frosty flight.

The Crystal Cocktail

In a glass of ice and flair,
Sparkles dance without a care.
Whispers swirl, a frosty tease,
Chilling tales upon the breeze.

Jokes with snowflakes take the stage,
Dramatic flair, an icy rage.
A twirl of frost, a laugh so bright,
Frozen fun in the evening light.

Secrets Hidden in Snowdrifts

Beneath the white, secrets unfold,
Tales of laughter, bright and bold.
Snowmen gossip, hats askew,
Chilly tales of me and you.

Sleds race down with gleeful shouts,
In winter's play, there's joy no doubt.
Earmuffs on, we spin around,
In snowy kingdoms, fun is found.

A Chill to Remember

Let's gather round the frosty flame,
To share a laugh, to play a game.
A chilly breeze, a playful sigh,
With snow as our confetti, oh my!

Frozen poses, each one grand,
Winter's acting, oh so planned.
A misstep here, a slip on snow,
Laughter rings as spirit's glow.

The Tempest in the Tundra

A whirl of snow, a frosty spin,
Drama brews as tempests begin.
Snowflakes frown, their dance so wild,
While giggles soar, the cold's beguiled.

Chilling winds with comic glee,
Spin the tale like a puppet spree.
In the tundra's embrace, we play,
Funny faces in winter's ballet.

Twinkle and Tumble

In a world of twinkling lights,
She twirled in sequined delight.
Her frosty crown, a little askew,
Oh, what a sight to view!

With every slip, she gave a shout,
'Is this a dance? Or am I out?'
Her flurry of flair, a charming mess,
How can one not admire this dress?

Hiccups of Ice

A hiccup here, a flutter there,
She sparkled, gasping for fresh air.
Her icy breath, a chilly puff,
'Beware the hiccup!' she cried, tough stuff!

With laughter, her friends join the spree,
Hiccups turn into a dance decree.
They jostled and jiggled on frozen ground,
Creating a ruckus, so funny and loud!

The Frozen Spotlight

Under the stars, she claimed the stage,
With ice in her veins, she turned the page.
A twinkling star in a dazzling gown,
Making her mark, she stood alone in the town.

But as she danced, a gust blew by,
Her fabulous flair took to the sky.
Though glam was lost in the chilly breeze,
She tossed her head back, laughing with ease!

Glistening Outrage

She stomped her foot, demanding glitz,
'No more plain snow, it's time for blitz!'
A snowball fight that turned to a brawl,
With laughter and giggles, they conquered it all.

Amidst the frosty drama and cheer,
Her antics, they piled up year after year.
Eccentric moves and icy flair,
A sweet delight that filled the air!

The Icy Masquerade Ball

In a frosty gown of white,
With sparkles shining bright,
She twirled on frosty floors,
Her crown made of ice, no wars.

The guests all slipped and slid,
With each frosty little bid,
Her laughter filled the room,
As snowflakes danced, a plume.

She wore a mask of frost,
But she was never lost,
With drama in her heart,
This night was just the start.

Her icy drama played on,
As winter's chill carried on,
With every wink and sigh,
She stole the show, oh my!

Glacial Passions Unfold

On a stage of snow and ice,
She acts with flair so nice,
Each tear froze mid-fall,
A sight to see at all.

The audience gasped, then laughed,
At every icy craft,
She tossed her scarf with flair,
A chill upon the air.

With every breath, a puff,
In her world, it's quite tough,
But she danced in the fray,
Sparking joy every day.

Oh the capers, the twists,
Her frosty plot, it insists,
With a wink and a glance,
She leads us in a dance.

Tales from the Chilling Stage

In a realm where frost was king,
A tale of laughs we bring,
With icy costumes worn,
For every heart that's torn.

She stomped and twirled with flair,
Sending shivers through the air,
With witty quips and jests,
She gave her fans the best.

Her antics bright as snow,
Stealing scenes with her glow,
Each mishap made them cheer,
In the cold, she drew them near.

In laughter, her heart would bloom,
Disguised within the gloom,
She spun a yarn so fun,
This chilly queen had won.

Caprice of the Cold

With a flip of icy hair,
And a chilly, frosty glare,
She stepped into the light,
Her regal heart ignites.

This queen knew how to play,
In her frosty kind of way,
Every laugh, a snowball flight,
Each drama, pure delight.

With every slip and fall,
She conquered one and all,
With giggles in the breeze,
She brought us all to freeze.

At the end of each cold jest,
With warmth, she'd gently rest,
For in her heart, we find,
The frosty queen is kind.

Sleds and Shadows

On a hill, the sleds do gleam,
A race is planned—a winter dream.
With laughter bright and spirits high,
We soar like birds beneath the sky.

A shadow slips, a twist, a turn,
Through snowflakes bright, our hearts will burn.
With every bump, a giggle bursts,
In frosty fun, we face the firsts.

Oh, who will fall? Oh, who will glide?
With joy we tumble side by side.
Each crash, a laugh, melodious cheer,
In this ice-bound world, we've nothing to fear.

As twilight falls, the challenge ends,
With rosy cheeks, we are all friends.
In the glow of dusk, with one last ride,
We dash down hills, adrenaline our guide.

The Dazzling Disguise

In the yard, a figure stands,
Wrapped in snow and waving hands.
A costume grand, a fashion spree,
Winter's ball, as bright as can be.

With carrot nose and buttons bright,
A sparkly scarf, oh what a sight!
The neighbors stare, their jaws drop low,
What kind of show is this in the snow?

They dance around, they sing and shout,
"Oh, look at that! What's it about?"
The chilly star starts to prance,
In frozen boots, it starts to dance.

The night wears thin, the laughter grows,
Who knew snow could put on shows?
A dazzling cloak in frosty air,
Creating smiles everywhere!

Snowy Silhouettes

In the moonlight, shadows creep,
Snowy forms that make us leap.
With each hush, a giggle grows,
What will pop up? Nobody knows!

A snowman here, a penguin there,
Chasing shapes with frosty flair.
A waltz of figures swirling round,
In snowy night, pure joy is found.

Kicking up the powdery flakes,
Giggles echo as the laughter wakes.
With every twist and every glide,
We dance along, our whimsical ride.

Embrace the night, let worries rest,
In playful glee, we are the best.
As snowflakes fall, they weave our tales,
In snowy silhouettes, our laughter sails.

Echoes Beneath the Snow

Beneath the frost, a secret lies,
Where whispers float and laughter flies.
A world aglow with snowy cheer,
Echoes of joy from far and near.

With every step, the echoes tease,
Dancing voices drift on the breeze.
"For every snow," the children cheer,
"Comes laughter, love, and winter's deer!"

Old boots crunch, new stories thrive,
In this sparkling world, we feel alive.
Round every corner, in every throw,
Are giggles bright beneath the snow.

As shadows stretch and daylight wanes,
We gather close, none has remains.
In memory's glow, our hearts embrace,
In echoes soft, we find our place.

Dramatic Polar Opposites

In the winter's chill, she steals the show,
A snowflake diva, with a flair to glow.
With every gust, she flounces around,
An ice-capped star, oh what a sound!

She shivers and twirls, a frosty pirouette,
While the crowd laughs on, they'll never forget.
With a wink and a spin, she makes all the fuss,
In winter's grand play, she's a must-see, thus!

The Winter Revelry

The grand gala comes when the snow starts to fall,
She enters the room, and it's a free-for-all.
With scarves and hats, they dance in delight,
This winter queen's laughter sparkles so bright.

Her snowman entourage steals the scene,
In a choreographed number, brisk and keen.
With a flip and a shimmy, they twirl with glee,
In this frosty soirée, wild jubilee!

Fickle Flurries

She flits like a flake, unpredictable and bold,
One moment she's warm, the next she's ice cold.
With a toss of her gloves, she stirs up a cheer,
Then melts into puddles, oh dear, oh dear!

But wait, there's more, she's back in a flash,
Wearing the sunset in a shimmering sash.
She loves all the drama, the laughter, the play,
This frosty maven, takes winter away!

Frigid Tale of Two Hearts

In a wintery world, where giggles take flight,
Two hearts meet and dance, in the pale moonlight.
One's dressed in snowflakes, the other in sleet,
Together they swirl in a frosty retreat.

But oh, the misunderstandings that freeze in the air,
With snowball exchanges and flurries to share.
Yet laughter erupts, as they melt the divide,
In this chilly romance, there's nowhere to hide!

Enchantments Under Ice

In the moonlit glimmer, he strikes a pose,
With a top hat and scarf, he steals the show.
Frost flakes dance, a chorus so bright,
Turning the stage into a winter delight.

He twirls like a diva, with flair and with grace,
But watch out for winter, that cold, icy face!
He sparkles and glistens, a shimmering sight,
Yet slips on a snowdrift, oh what a fright!

His buddies laugh loud, while he takes a spill,
With snowballs in hand, they climb up the hill.
They toss and they tumble, what a wild scene,
As laughter erupts for our snowy machine!

In this enchanted frost, where the snowflakes fall,
He reigns as the king, though he trips once and all.
A magical tale of fun in the cold,
With antics and flurries, it's priceless, untold!

The Chilly Dialogue

On a brisk winter's morn, they gather anew,
With snowflakes a-flying in a bright sky so blue.
Chatter and laughter, they boast and they brag,
As he dons a filled hat, his ego a flag.

"I'm quite the sensation," he declares with a wink,
"A snowman extraordinaire, more than you think!"
His friends roll their eyes, but they just play along,
For the banter and charm are what make them strong.

"You think you're so clever, with your frosty ballet?"
One friend smirks back, quite snarky today.
They tease and they jibe, in their chilly exchange,
As they slip and they slide, in a frosty range.

With snowballs and shivers, the jesting ensues,
While the sky overhead fills with wisps of soft hues.
In this crisp winter bloom, where giggles ignite,
The chilly dialogue dances from day into night!

The Mother of All Snowstorms

A storm is brewing, it's quite the affair,
With winds that are howling, and ice in the air.
He struts in the snowfall, all wild and grand,
Creating a blizzard, just as he planned.

The snow drifts around him, a flurry of flair,
While friends grab their sleds, excitement to share.
"Watch my sweet moves, as I glide through the chill!"
He tumbles and fumbles, giving everyone a thrill.

When the flakes are piled high, he calls out a cheer,
"I'm the star of this storm! Come and gather near!"
But just as he poses, he slips with a squeal,
And tumbles like thunder, oh what a reveal!

Yet laughter erupts, as he brushes the snow,
With a grin so bright, and a hearty 'Let's go!'
They ride down the hill, hearts light and carefree,
In this mother of storms, where all spirits agree!

Heartbreak and Harmony in White

In a snowy expanse, he gazes forlorn,
A love lost to winter, just as the sun's born.
With a heart made of ice and a sigh from the breeze,
He pines for the warmth with a feeling that freezes.

But wait, here comes laughter, a chorus anew,
His friends rally round him, in a joyful crew.
A snowball in hand and a wink in their eyes,
They lift his spirits high, as the snowflakes fly.

"Don't mope in the drifts, come join in the fun!"
"We'll build a great palace, there's plenty to run!"
Through plights and through giggles, the frosty heart sways,
As they craft a bright kingdom, through laughter-filled days.

In the heart of the storm, with friendships so bold,
He finds solace in snow, with a tale to be told.
For in frost and in cheer, through the chill and the chill,
Love's harmony grows, where heartaches are still.

Frigid Fits of Fancy

In a world of snowflakes, she prances so bold,
With a crown made of icicles, but oh, she gets cold.
She stomps and she twirls in her wintertime dress,
Telling tales of her frost that are nothing but mess.

Her laughter like crystals, it clinks in the air,
While her friends roll their eyes, they can't help but stare.
"Look at me!" she declares, as she slips on some ice,
Only to land in a tumble—oh, isn't that nice?

She throws frosty fits, oh what a delight,
Pouting and pouting 'til the end of the night.
But when she stops whining and glimmers with glee,
The frosty facade fades, she's as fun as can be!

So here's to the one who's as chilly as steam,
With dreams full of snowflakes, each one unique theme.
In the drama-filled winter, she steals every scene,
Our queen of the cold, she reigns ever keen.

Glittering Injustice

In a sparkly town where the ice castles gleam,
Lies a diva of winter, the queen of her dream.
With a flair for theatrics, she always demands,
That the snowflakes all follow her glittery plans.

With a flick of her wrist and a wave of her hand,
She claims every snowman, declares she's the brand.
"These snowballs are mine!" she proclaims with a pout,
As the others roll by with their laughter throughout.

Her costumes of sparkle, so lavish, so bright,
Yet each gust of wind sends her twirling in fright.
"Who dares to distract me while I'm making my art?"
The ice bunnies giggle and roll from the start.

Yet in her grand chaos, a charm still shines through,
For drama brings laughter—who knew it was true?
Though she battles for center stage each frosty dawn,
We can't help but love her—this drama-queen spawn.

Crystal Clashes

Underneath the starlight, where the glaciers collide,
There's a drama unfolding, with nowhere to hide.
A battle of snowflakes, so fierce and so bright,
Our frosty protagonist sparks mischievous fright.

With a scepter of ice, she demands all the fun,
Screaming, "I'm fabulous!" while hiding her run.
While shivering reindeer are rolling their eyes,
Coz when she takes center stage, it's chaos that lies.

Each step is a statement, each twirl's a grand show,
She makes sure the spotlight is always aglow.
Like a snowstorm her tantrums explode and they swirl,
These crystal top clashes leave heads in a whirl.

But beneath all the glitz, there's warmth in her heart,
With laughter and mischief, she's a true work of art.
Each freeze frame a memory, each fall a delight,
In her frosty kingdom, the world feels just right.

The Icy Stage

On a stage built of ice, with a sparkle so bright,
Our frosty actress twirls into the limelight.
"I'm the fairest of them!" with a grin and a spin,
While gumdrops and snowflakes go flying like sin.

With props made of snow, she takes her grand stance,
In a flurry of antics, she leads the expanse.
A meltdown of laughter, her nibbled-up toes
Escape to the moonlight, where everything glows.

As flurries of giggles rise high in the air,
It's impossible not to succumb to her flair.
In her world of the chilly, she rules with such grace,
The wintertime drama is her favorite place.

So let the shows go on, let the ice crystals shine,
In the heart of the cold, she glimmers divine.
Each seasoned performance is one for the books,
This queen of the frosty, oh, just take a look!

Echoes of a Winter Star

A snowman draped in silk attire,
Bows and ribbon piled with fire.
With a scarf that's far too long,
She twirls and sings her frosty song.

A haughty flap of fake fur coat,
She strikes a pose on icy moat.
Giggles float on chilled out air,
As winter folks just stop and stare.

With twinkling eyes and great aplomb,
She claims the stage and brings the calm.
But with a wink, she tips the show,
And all her plans just go aglow.

In frosty breath she fans her hair,
As snowflakes shiver everywhere.
A diva in the frozen scene,
Who takes the lead in all her sheen.

Glittering Glares and Chilly Stares

Underneath a snowy crown,
She stomps about the little town.
With glimmer beads hanging tight,
She banishes the dull delight.

Her icy glare from frozen gates,
Keeps everyone from rolling waits.
With every flip of her bright fan,
The wind conspires to her grand plan.

She flicks her nose with a frosty glee,
And the crowd gasps, "What will it be?"
Dramatic sighs and flouncy skirts,
Make jaws drop, despite the squirts.

In slopes of snow, they laugh and play,
While she holds court in every way.
The queen of flakes, the frost of fun,
With each grand act, she's never done.

The Frostbitten Leading Lady

Oops! Her nose fell off one night,
But does she care? It's still alright.
With red cheeks and a twinkling grin,
The best of shows is about to begin.

Glitters rain with every move,
A pirouette to make you groove.
She waves her arms like winter's breeze,
And everyone bows down with ease.

Each flake that lands on cheeks so cold,
Her antics bold, her heart of gold.
With a pirouette and a flustered sigh,
She steals the breath from the passing sky.

Such grand emotions packed with fun,
In a play beneath the winter sun.
An actress born from snow and light,
Her frosty heart, a pure delight.

Frost and Fury on the Stage

The glint of ice, a fiery chase,
She dances in her cool embrace.
With every twirl, a chilly laugh,
The crowd applauds her snowy craft.

Her icy jokes and winter schemes,
Make every snowman giggle in dreams.
With a flip and swirl and fierce finesse,
She frolics boldly in winter's dress.

But on this stage of snow and frost,
Seems even she has moments tossed.
A slip, a trip, the audience roars,
As she recovers and then implores.

With a wink and twinkling cheer,
She lives for joy, let's all draw near!
The frosty queen with a heart so bright,
Turns every chill into pure delight.

Melodies of the Frozen

In the land of chilly cheer,
A figure prances, bringing fear.
With a flip and a spin, she starts to glow,
All eyes are on her, stealing the show.

Her nose a carrot, her crown of ice,
She twirls and twirls, so very nice.
But watch your step, don't slip or slide,
Her drama's grand, she takes it in stride.

With each frosty gust, her wig takes flight,
She squeals and shimmies, what a sight!
"Take my photograph; my good side, please!"
Her antics make the cold winds freeze.

"Oh, dear crowd, would you clap for me?"
As snowflakes dance to her decree.
In a whirlwind of laughter, she leaps and spins,
In the frosty realm, let the fun begin!

A Chill of Wild Emotions

In a snowglobe world, she holds a throne,
Crafting narratives from ice and bone.
With every frost and chilly breath,
She acts like winter's leading guest.

"Why so serious?" the icicles tease,
She pouts and twirls with the greatest of ease.
Her heart's a blizzard, emotions run high,
Hearts melt away under her icy sigh.

Ice skates gleam as she takes a leap,
Beneath the surface, secrets to keep.
With sparkly shards and glittery flair,
Her chilly passion fills the air.

"Applause, my darlings!" she sings with glee,
As snowmen roll their eyes, carefree.
In this frozen spectacle, she's the star,
Who knew cold could carry such bizarre?

Daze of Frost and Fracture

The frosty queen with a twisty crown,
Winks and giggles, never a frown.
But shards of ice break with each flail,
"Oh dear! Watch out! Be cautious, or fail!"

With a flounce and a stomp, she claims her space,
Leaping high in a sparkling lace.
"Oh look! An avalanche of laughter awaits,"
She ducks and dives, casting off weights.

But brr, it's cold, her fingers freeze,
Still she dances, full of tease.
"Just one more act," she daintily cries,
Ignoring the snowballs flying by.

Her world's a stage, frosty and bright,
A winter cabaret of sheer delight.
"Make room for magic!" she shouts with glee,
In this joy-filled chaos, surely she'll be!

Raindrops and Snowflakes

Raindrops fall as she takes her bow,
Sparkling laughter pushes through the cold now.
"Twirling in puddles, I'm a queen today!"
She juggles snowflakes, come join the fray!

With a playful wink and a dash of flair,
She conjures up fun, filling the air.
"Bring out the bubbles, and bring out the cheer! "
In her frosty kingdom, all is held dear.

The frost bites lightly, yet she prances on,
While rain starts to sprinkle, she's never withdrawn.
"Let's dance in this storm, join this delight!"
With every clap, the world feels just right.

Snowflakes swirl, merging with rain,
Her heart beats wildly, boundless and plain.
"Can't stop this fun, not now, not ever!"
As puddles form, her spirit's a clever!

The Bravado of a Winter Muse

In a flurry of sparkles, she takes the stage,
A diva in white, with a frosty rage.
Her scarf is a banner, her hat a crown,
A pirouette here, and the world turns upside down.

With a twinkle and giggle, she throws her flair,
In the world of snowflakes, she dances with care.
The trees stand in awe, with branches aglow,
This snow-laden queen knows just how to steal the show.

She winks at the sun as it peeks from the clouds,
While the children laugh, forming curious crowds.
With the breeze in her hair, she lets out a squeal,
Who knew that a chill could feel this surreal?

As her laughter echoes, the earth holds its breath,
In a crafty display that teases sweet death.
Oh, the winter's a stage, it's a whimsical scene,
All thanks to the flair of this frosty routine.

Slumbering Under a Shroud of Snow

The world is asleep in a fluffy embrace,
A blanket of white, not a single trace.
She twirls in her dreams, draped in sheer chill,
With a wink and a grin, she has time to kill.

Cuddled close by, the snowflakes agree,
Each flake is a star in this quiet spree.
As the night takes hold, she hums low and sweet,
In her frostbitten kingdom, her heart skips a beat.

With a glimmer of mischief, she teases the freeze,
Whispering stories in the cold winter breeze.
Her laughter dances like snow upon ground,
In the silence of frost, joy's awaiting, unbound.

Beneath her soft shroud, all the dozing folks dream,
That winter's a caper, not just what it seems.
In the deep of night, under chilly delight,
This queen of the freeze spins her tales soft and bright.

The Chill that Captivates

She struts through the darkness, a glimmering sprite,
A master of drama in the dead of night.
With an attitude bold, she sashays away,
In a tempest of giggles, she frolics and plays.

The frost gathers round her, a shimmering crowd,
As she takes her bow, feeling blissfully proud.
Each icicle sparkles, a diamond in tow,
A queen to the cold air, with a colorful glow.

The wind starts to whistle, a chorus in song,
As she prances and twirls, nothing seems wrong.
With glances of mischief and sparkles of cheer,
She conquers the season with laughter sincere.

Oh, the chill lifts her high, on a throne made of snow,
In a spectacle bright, where the breezy winds blow.
With the night as her stage and the stars as her bright,
She captures the chill, in this frosty delight.

Heartstrings in a Frosty Episode

With a puff of her cheeks, she creates a soft mist,
A clever little play, you can't help but twist.
In a symphony chilly, she winks at the moon,
This frosty affair is a whimsical tune.

Her laughter cascades like the snow from the trees,
In the heart of the winter, she moves with the breeze.
Wrapped up in a swirl, she delights with a cheer,
As snowflakes join in on her cue—oh, so dear!

With a hop and a skip, she embraces the cold,
Each step is a story, each laugh is pure gold.
Through the giggles and warmth that her spirit does bring,
Even snowmen are grinning, at the joy she can fling.

In her frosted escape, every heart starts to play,
Juggling snowballs and dreams in a merry ballet.
With her charm and her sparkle, she sings without fright,
In a world that's enchanted, by this frosty delight.

Avalanche of Emotions

In a world of snowflakes' dance,
A heart lets out a frozen glance.
With teardrops like icicles, she sighs,
Her frosty antics bring surprise.

Amidst the chill, she'll pout and play,
In the winter's chilly ballet.
With every twist and every turn,
She's the star, let her heart burn!

Snowmen laugh at her dismay,
As winter's winds do shout and sway.
Her costume sparkles in the light,
But the cold turns giggles to fright!

Oh, the layers she must wear,
To cope with this icy affair!
An avalanche of laughter rolls,
Through her frosty, shining soul.

The Frostbite Fiasco

In a blizzard, she took the stage,
With drama that could fill a page.
Her glitter sparkled, oh so bright,
Yet clouds above brought endless fright.

Chilly winds would howl in jest,
"Why not wear a warmer vest?"
But sequins twinkled, bold and grand,
She won't yield to winter's hand!

With a flip of her snow-white mane,
She slipped and fell, a whimsical bane.
The crowd erupted, laughter soared,
As she acted, the frost adored!

Through frosty flops, she's full of glee,
A winter queen, wild and free.
In every stumble, she finds grace,
Her icy heart's true, shining place.

Sparkling Sorrow

Glittering tears dripped like hail,
In her frosty, joyful tale.
With every flake, a new lament,
She spins her woes, a cold descent.

Her heart a glacier, hard and bright,
In the spotlight, a dazzling sight.
She twirls in circles, spills her pain,
A snowstorm dance, quite insane!

A crown of ice above her head,
With every jest, a frosty shred.
Yet in her laughter, sorrow gleams,
Caught in the web of winter's dreams.

Through sparkling sorrow, full of cheer,
She sparkles bright, though shadows near.
A queen of frost, in laughter bound,
Her chilly jests resound around.

Glacial Glamour

Oh, what a sight, so bold and bright,
With glacial glamour, pure delight.
She struts with flair, a frozen grace,
In a feld of winter's embrace.

Her laughter echoes, crisp and clear,
While others quake in chilling fear.
With every step, a frosty cheer,
The drama queen, we hold so dear.

A party waits, for winter's show,
Her glimmering gown steals the blow.
Though winter's bite may come for free,
In glacial glamour, she's carefree.

With humor bright as snow's white glare,
She dances lightly in the air.
For with each giggle, the cold retreats,
As frosty charm and laughter meet!

Glamour in the Gloom

In a world of white and gray,
She struts with flair, come what may.
With a scarf of sparkly frost,
She's the toast of the snowy coast.

Her hat sits askew, a crown of ice,
With every flake, she's oh so nice.
The chill might bite, but she'll survive,
With style and sass, she comes alive.

Neighbors gasp at her winter glow,
As she twirls about in the falling snow.
Making snow angels with impeccable grace,
Who knew winter could hold such a face?

But watch out for her haughty flair,
A snowball fight? Oh, she'll declare!
With a wink, she takes careful aim,
In this wintry stage, it's all a game.

The Icebound Debacle

With a twirl and a skip, she made her stand,
Flaunting bling in this icy land.
Her frozen tiara shone bright,
In a battle of snow, no fear in sight.

The villagers watched, ready to cheer,
As she spilled drama, loud and clear.
But a snowman grinned, the odds were stacked,
Her grand show might just be hacked!

She slipped on her cape, all fluffy and bold,
Bounced back, her antics uncontrolled.
The crowd roared with laughter and glee,
In this frosty mess, she danced with spree.

With glamour and giggles, the tale was spun,
Her icy escapade, all in good fun.
A diva on ice, she'd not be beat,
In the frosty chaos, she found her seat.

Chilling Elegance

Amid snowflakes, she makes her way,
Draped in white, oh such a play.
With a twinkling laugh and a whimsical sway,
Chilling elegance, leading the fray.

The cold wind didn't faze her hair,
Glistening curls of frosty flair.
Her laughter echoed through the chilly air,
As she danced 'round like she didn't care.

But the frosty ground had tales to weave,
One slip, and all would grieve!
Yet with a wink and a carefree toss,
She spun around, a winner, not a loss.

Onlookers cheered, "What a scene!"
For this frosty queen, so pristine.
In the winter warmth, she carved her part,
A dazzling show that melted hearts!

The Snowball Effect

With a flick of her wrist, she's ready to blast,
Snowballs flying, oh, what a contrast!
Puffs of white fly through the air,
As laughter bubbles everywhere.

She shouts, "Take that!" with dramatic flair,
Pirouetting in her frozen chair.
A snowball lands right on her nose,
Before she bursts into giggles and throws!

The crowd joins in, a charming affair,
Each flurry of fun, a wintry dare.
They tumble and roll, all with delight,
In a frosted frenzy that lasts all night.

Controlled chaos, oh what a game,
With giggles and shrieks to stake their claim.
As the sun sets low, their antics ignite,
In the snowball effect, pure joy takes flight.

Chilling Adventures of a Bold Performer

In a costume fit for the show,
With sparkles and flair in tow.
A sassy strut and a frozen pout,
On stage, there's never a doubt!

Twirling on ice, she spins with grace,
A spotlight shining on her face.
With every fall, the giggles grow,
The audience loves this frosty glow!

Her cape flies high like a snowy kite,
In winter wonder, she steals the night.
With drama thick in each chilly scene,
A laugh-out-loud, bold routine!

So gather 'round for a comical tale,
Of a snowy star who'll never pale.
With each twist, snag, and playful shout,
She's the frosty diva we can't live without!

A Thespian's Frozen Fate

A butterfly trapped in a frozen mist,
On stage, the performers can't resist.
With layers of warmth and a snazzy hat,
The audience waits for the next little spat.

In her heart, she feels the heat,
But outside, the chill can't be beat.
A slapstick skit with snowball props,
Laughing so hard, no one ever stops!

Behind the curtain, the whispers spread,
What antics await? What chaos ahead?
With every line, a back-flip or spin,
In her frosty world, she just can't win!

So here's to the star with a flair for fun,
In a chilly play, she's second to none.
With gusto and giggles, she steals the night,
A frosty thespian in laughter's light!

Snowdrift Epiphanies

In a blizzard of sparkles with laughter in air,
Through frosty drifts, she'll dance without care.
Her big frosty heart beats loud with delight,
As she prances and twirls in the pale moonlight.

A snowman sidekick, always in line,
With a carrot nose and a smirk so divine.
They sashay and slip on the icy tiled floor,
Sharing the love as they tumble and roar!

With grand proclamations from snowy-peaked hills,
The drama unfolds with whimsical thrills.
In each chilly twist, her charm ignites,
A wintery show filled with frosty delights!

As laughter erupts, the audience cheers,
Boundless joy melts away all their fears.
So here's to the fun in a snowy-spun dream,
Where frosty moments are more than they seem!

Shattered Glass and Crystal Tears

The stage is set with a glimmering sheen,
Ice sculptures looming like a frosty queen.
With a wry little wink, she slips on her dress,
And the audience waits for her dramatic mess.

A curtain rise reveals a sight so grand,
With epic flops, she can hardly stand!
A whirlwind of laughter as props go awry,
Crystal tears freeze, but she won't say goodbye!

The music kicks in, a jazzy surprise,
With every misstep, she plays it wise.
In a flurry of giggles, she takes the fall,
And the audience roars, they're having a ball!

Through shattered glass, she finds her cue,
A frosty lesson, in laughter's view.
With wit so sharp and a spirit so bright,
She twirls through the chaos, a comical night!

Whispers of Winter Woe

In a frosted world, she takes her stage,
With snowflake flair, she turns each page.
Glittering bobbles glitter in the light,
She twirls and shimmies, a vibrant sight.

Her frosty breath sends the warm hearts racing,
Complaints about chill, quite oft she's facing.
With every sigh, the cold winds wail,
In pink and blue, she tells her tale.

Each snowman grins, they know her charm,
Beneath her antics, there's a warmth, not harm.
With every flake, she throws a show,
That wins the audience, row by row.

But winter scowls, with humor bold,
Her antics too bright, her laughs too cold.
She lifts the gloom, makes dark skies beam,
In her frosty world, they're trapped in a dream.

The Frosted Castaway

An icy adventurer, she's lost at sea,
With frosty curls, and her sassy glee.
Lamenting her wardrobe, "Where's my coat?"
She chuckles to seagulls, a weird old quote.

Snow drifts dance around her toes,
With a wink and a flip, as she strikes a pose.
She summons the snowflakes, makes them swirl,
Each twirl is magic, as her jacket unfurl.

The waves hurl laughter, they tumble and crash,
While she trips on frigid ice, her notes a smash.
"Oh dear ocean, I'll make you my friend,
With giggles and sprinkles, let the fun never end!"

In a frosted beach party, she bakes in the sun,
Her mittens a laugh, in a world full of fun.
With every wave crashing, the cold winds play,
The frosted castaway dances away.

Chilling Charades

She strikes a pose in the winter's glow,
Of frozen delights, she steals the show.
With each icy shimmy, she dares to bring,
A comical charm, like a puppet on string.

She mimics the snowmen, with noses of carrot,
Hopping and twisting, but lacking the merit.
"Oh, look at me! I'm icy and bold!"
They giggle and snicker, as the story unfolds.

With marshmallow hats, and cocoa in hand,
She hosts a great party, the best in the land.
Guests made of snow, they dance and they clap,
While she takes her bow, in a fluffy white cap.

Yet, when the sun shines, she feels bittersweet,
For melting away is her greatest defeat.
But in every moment, hilarity springs,
In chilling charades, she's the queen of the flings.

Ice Queen's Lament

In her mirror of frost, she rehearses her face,
A sparkle of mischief, with an icy grace.
"Oh woe," she sighs, "why can't they see?
I'm the beauty of winter, wild and free!"

With cada twirl, she feigns oh so grand,
Pretending to care, but lacking a hand.
"The colder, the better," she laughs with a cheer,
As snowflakes pray, "Oh, keep her near!"

She spreads winter's charm, with a wink and a laugh,
Strumming on icicles, a chilly craft.
But her tears fall softly, like frost on the pond,
For in every joke, a softness beyond.

Yet, humor remains, and she dances away,
"Just watch me on stage, come laugh, come play!"
In her kingdom of frost, with giggles and cheer,
The ice queen will reign, throughout the year.

Stages of Snow and Heartbreak

In the quiet of a winter's night,
A figure twirls, looking just right.
With each flake that falls, tears may gleam,
But oh dear, it's all part of the dream.

Sauntering past, they strike a pose,
Wishing for love while in freezing throes.
A snowball fight turns into a scene,
Oh, the heartbreak of this chilled routine!

Dramatic sighs fill the frosty air,
As icy breath escapes in despair.
With each slip and trip, quite the display,
A king or queen in the snow ballet.

Through laughter and slips, the fun won't cease,
These winter whispers bring a sense of peace.
For in the flurry, we find our role,
In snow's embrace, let's free our soul.

The Enchanted Winter Soliloquy.

On a cold stage, the spotlight beams,
With sparkling white, like fairy dreams.
A prima donna in a scarf so bright,
Enacting a tale in the pale moonlight.

"My heart is cold, my love, so true!"
Each snowflake falling plays a cue.
With a toss of her hat, she pouts just right,
A scene so comical, a comedic fright.

With snowman extras, they join the play,
In silly costumes, giggling all day.
She flings a handful of snow in a rage,
Oh, the drama unfolds on this winter stage!

But soon laughter overcomes the frown,
As snowflakes gather to shake her down.
In this enchanted winter, hearts freeze and thaw,
Each giggle and slip, a perfect encore.

Snowflake Serenades

A flurry swirls, a dance begins,
With snowflakes swirling like twirling wins.
Oh, she shimmies and shakes, a frosty display,
As each flake whispers, "Come out to play!"

Her scarf wrapped tight, looking chic yet bold,
In a drama of chill that never gets old.
With a wink and a laugh, she sings to the sky,
"Catch me if you can, I'm too cool to lie!"

She spins in circles, trails of white lace,
A humorous queen in this frozen space.
And as the frostbite nips at her nose,
She giggles aloud, her happiness glows.

In the soft light of dawn, she takes a bow,
To her winter symphony, she says, "I vow!"
With laughter and joy as the melody plays,
This snowflake serenade brightens our days.

Glittering Meltdowns

Under the stars, in the icy scene,
A tipsy twirl, oh how it's been!
Her sequined dress glints like the frost,
Each pirouette a moment lost.

With a flick of her wrist, she summons the snow,
A sparkling world where giggles flow.
But oh, with a slip, she tumbles down,
A glittering meltdown, in laughter she drowns!

The audience laughs, applauding her fall,
A comedic queen, she charmed them all.
She stands back up, a grin on her face,
Ready to dance in this wintery place.

In the chilly night, her heart it glows,
For in every mishap, the merriment grows.
So let's raise our cups to the frosty spree,
Where glittering meltdowns are meant to be free.

The Slippery Slicker

In a coat of shimmering white,
With a twirl, he takes flight.
His icy grin, a cheeky tease,
Sprinkling snow with every breeze.

He slips and slides with flair so grand,
Waving to the people and the band.
With a wink, he starts to glide,
In his frosty, chilly pride.

He shouts, 'Watch me catch this freeze!'
With a dash, he bends the knees.
Dropping down, he's shoving snow,
Creating drama in the show.

But oops! A fall, so swift and slick,
He tumbles down, quite the trick.
With laughter ringing through the air,
He jumps back up, beyond compare.

Winter's Enchanted Revue

On the stage of frozen dreams,
Where the sparkle brightly beams.
A twinkle here, a shimmy there,
He dances with an icy flair.

The spotlight shines on frosty cheeks,
A performance full of squeaks.
With each jest and playful spin,
The crowd erupts, he's sure to win!

He leaps and bounds in snowflake shoes,
Transforming cold into great news.
Oh, the giggles and stomps abound,
As laughter echoes all around.

But wait! A slip, a frosty quake,
His grand finale, a giant wake.
He lands with flair, a snowy pile,
And all just laugh and love his style.

Dramatic Flurries and Daring Twirls

With a flourish and a swoosh,
He dances in the freezing hush.
Flurries swirl and tumble round,
As he twirls without a sound.

His cape of snow, a billowing sheet,
Makes every move a grand repeat.
He strikes a pose, looks oh so bold,
In this winter tale, he's uncontrolled.

Like a leaf upon the breeze,
He does as he pleases with such ease.
The drama unfolds in snowy delight,
As he gives the season a cheery fright.

But right on cue, a gust comes through,
He flails and spins, oh what a view!
With a giggle, he lands in the drifts,
A crown of snow, as laughter lifts.

The Icebound Muse's Lament

Upon the stage of ice so clear,
He whispers tales, all ears, come near.
With a regal flair, he does bemoan,
The winter chill, yet feels at home.

His voice, a comedy wrapped in frost,
With every line, no moment lost.
"Oh dear audience, hear my plight!"
He bounds with flair, all merry and light.

He pleads with snowflakes, 'Join my quest,
Let's show them all, we're the best!'
With a twirl and a wink, he slays,
A winter prince in jest conveys.

Yet alas! The icy stage is slick,
He tries a leap, a frosty trick.
Down he goes with a startled yelp,
But laughter rings, it's part of the help.

Exquisite Winter Rants

Oh, look at me, I'm icy and grand,
With a glittery scarf, I'm making a stand!
The kids love to fashion their silly snowman,
But my fabulous flair? They just don't understand!

I'm prone to a meltdown, can't you tell?
When the sun shines bright, I bid farewell.
They build me up high, then watch me fall,
In this frosty parade, I'm the star of it all!

Drama in flurries, I dance with delight,
Chasing snowflakes, I'm ready for flight.
With a swirl and a twirl, I claim my domain,
The laughter and fun make me forget the disdain!

Wintertime antics, oh what a flair,
With a wink and a nod, I'm debonair.
So gather around, enjoy the cool breeze,
For I'm not just ice; I do as I please!

Caprices of the Cold

In my frosty attire, I strut with some sass,
Crisp air in my lungs, I'm a frosty brass.
With a snicker and jest, I challenge the freeze,
Turning snowball fights into great comedies!

A snowy charade, I twirl with a grin,
Echoes of giggles, let the chill begin!
But don't push my buttons, or I might just pout,
This sparkling queen has lots of clout!

Snowflakes conspire, they twinklingly tease,
I reign over winter, an ice-crowned tease.
With hot cocoa sips, I chuckle with cheer,
In this frosty realm, I'm ever so near!

So dance in the snow, let joy overflow,
Through whimsical winds, let your laughter blow.
In my capricious reign, let the good times unfold,
For life's just a stage when you're brash and cold!

Glimmering Resilience

With a glimmering gaze, I face the bleak night,
A snowy diva, bursting with light.
When life gets too chilly, I proudly proclaim,
Resilience in frost is my glorious game!

Though the frost nips at my perfectly styled 'do,
I strut through the turmoil, bold and true.
Each chilly gust sings a laughter-filled tune,
For I am the joy, winter's playful boon!

Sassy and sparkly, I saunter along,
Gathering giggles, where I belong.
With a wink and a shuffle on this icy spree,
I show them the strength of a cold jubilee!

So raise up your mugs, let the warmth stay inside,
For in glimmering winters, I shall abide.
Through waltzes of snow, I glide with finesse,
In the heart of the cold, I will always impress!

Shimmery Snowdrift Sagas

On a shimmery stage, where snowflakes will frolic,
Watch as I prance with my ice-crowned frolic.
Tickled by gusts, I frolic and sway,
In this shimmery tale, I'm bold every day!

Snowdrifts become cushions, I dive in with flair,
Reigning like royalty, without a care.
A boisterous laugh in the chill of the frost,
For I am the shimmer, never the lost!

Frosty whispers tell sagas untold,
With giggles as armor, I'm never too cold.
In a swirl of white, I orchestrate fun,
With a flair and a dash, I've already won!

So gather your friends for this frosty ballet,
Let the glittering tales take your blues far away.
In my whimsical world where the snowflakes dance high,

I'll reign as the jester 'neath the bright winter sky!

Frostbitten Fantasies

In a world of snowflakes, she twirls with flair,
Her icy breath hangs in the frosty air.
With a glimmer of mischief, she strikes a pose,
A prima donna beneath winter's prose.

Dressed in white fluff, like a snowy delight,
She steals the scene in the pale moonlight.
Her drama unfolds with each chilly gust,
Whispers of laughter mix with a touch of frost dust.

She twinkles and sparkles in glacial delight,
Creating a spectacle, oh, what a sight!
As giggles echo through the snowy domain,
Our frosty diva brings warmth in the rain.

So snowflakes shake off their wintery fright,
To dance in her shadow beneath twinkling light.
In a frosty performance that cheers up the night,
She reigns with a chuckle, a queen in her height.

Winter's Private Theater

In the theater of snow, she takes center stage,
With laughter and giggles, she sets the age.
Her voice like a whisper, a crisp winter's breeze,
Commands all attention with effortless ease.

The audience gathers, all creatures in awe,
As she dons her fine costume, a shimmering straw.
With a flick of her wrist, she tosses some snow,
And the laughter erupts, oh, how it will flow!

Each act brings a chuckle, a slip and a slide,
She glides through the scenes with a wink and a stride.
In a flurry of antics, our star takes a bow,
With icicles hanging like jewels on her brow.

As the curtain draws close on this cold winter's night,
She winks one last time, a frosty delight.
In winter's grand theater, she played her sweet part,
Leaving behind all a warm, giggly heart.

Heart of the Icicle

With a heart made of ice, she sets off to play,
Her antics so funny, they melt all the gray.
She dances and prances on rooftops so high,
Chasing down snowballs that whirl through the sky.

In a frosty ensemble, she captivates all,
Her laughter as bright as the snowfall's own call.
From igloos to snowmen, her charm runs the show,
Each cold winter moment brings giggles and glow.

Falling and tumbling, she bounces around,
Her heart of an icicle knows no bound.
Playfully tripping on her own two feet,
She shimmies through winter with radiant heat.

As she gathers her pals for a snowball fight,
The joy of the season shines ever so bright.
With snowflakes like feathers, they cheer and they cheer,
While the heart of the icicle warms us all near.

Shivering Spotlight

In the spotlight of winter, she shivers and shakes,
Stealing the show, making snow angels with flake.
Her comedic relief brings glimmers of joy,
A frosty sensation, that every girl and boy.

With her flurry of giggles, she bounces about,
Like a playful deer, with a gleeful shout.
Her breath forms a cloud that spells out the fun,
As she dances through snowbanks, her show has begun.

Each tumble and twist is a comedic delight,
As she flips through the air in the shimmering night.
With a smile like sunshine, she warms up the scene,
Our frosty performer, the bold winter queen.

So gather around for her frosty charade,
In this shivering spotlight, let laughter cascade.
With snowflakes and giggles, she brings us all cheer,
A diva of winter, our hearts she will steer.